OTHER BOOKS BY HELEN EXLEY:

Over 50s' Jokes	**Cat Jokes**
Over 60s' Jokes	**365 Happy Days!**
Over 70s' Jokes	**Senior Moments 365**
Over 80s' Jokes	**Life! And other disasters... 365**

EDITED BY HELEN EXLEY

Published in 2019 by Helen Exley ®LONDON in Great Britain.
Design, selection and arrangement © Helen Exley Creative Ltd 2019.
Illustrated by Roland Fiddy © Helen Exley Creative Ltd 2019.
All the words by Peter Gray, Pam Brown, Helen Thomson
copyright © Helen Exley Creative Ltd 2019.
The moral rights of the authors have been asserted.

12 11 10 9 8 7 6 5 4 3 2 1

ISBN: 978-1-78485-237-5

Helen Exley ® LONDON,
16 Chalk Hill, Watford, Herts WD19 4BG, UK
www.helenexley.com

Golf
Jokes

CARTOONS BY ROLAND FIDDY

Helen Exley

"Say, Caddie, why do you keep
looking at your watch?"
"It isn't a watch, Sir, it's a compass."

AUTHOR UNKNOWN

Golf is a good

Not a week goes by without my learning
something new about golf. That means,
of course, that I was ignorant of eight
things about golf two months ago.
Extend that process back nearly twenty
years and the result is an impressive
accumulation of ignorance.

PETER DOBEREINER

walk spoiled.

MARK TWAIN

Handicap: An allocation of strokes
on one or more holes that permits
two golfers of very different ability
to do equally poorly on the same course.

HENRY BEARD AND ROY MCKIE

...the course designers and the pros
are in collusion.
One is paid to drive you mad
by making the course impossible.
The other is paid to drive you mad
teaching you how to overcome
the obstacles that shouldn't
have been there in the first place.

HELEN RICHARDS

All games are silly,
but golf, if you look at it
dispassionately,
goes to extremes.

PETER ALLISS

"So, the judge
fined you fifty dollars
for hitting that man
with a club?"
"Oh, it wasn't so much
for hitting him
as it was for using
the wrong club."

AUTHOR UNKNOWN

I never exaggerate. I just remember big.

CHI CHI RODRIGUEZ

Golf:

A game in which a ball
one and half inches in diameter
is placed on a ball 8,000 miles
in diameter.
The object is to hit the small ball
but not the larger.

JOHN CUNNINGHAM

If you're caught on a golf course
during a storm and
you are afraid of lightning,
hold up a 1-iron.
Not even God can hit a 1-iron.

LEE TREVINO

A cardinal rule
for the club breaker
is never to break
your putter and driver
in the same match
or you are dead.

TOMMY BOLT

I get upset over a bad shot
just like anyone else.
But it's silly to let the game
get to you. When I miss a shot
I just think what a beautiful day
it is. And what pure fresh air
I'm breathing. Then I take
a deep breath. I have to do that.
That's what gives me
the strength to break the club.

BOB HOPE

For some people it is simply life –
liberty, and the pursuit of a golf ball.

AUTHOR UNKNOWN

Golfers play golf to prove
that they can mentally overcome
the pressures that golf puts upon them.
The fact that if they didn't
play golf at all they would not
have to endure or overcome
its pressures may not occur to them.

PETER GAMMOND

Nothing goes down slowe

han a golf handicap.

BOBBY NICHOLS

Ruining yet another shot,
the duffer whimpered,
"There can't be worse players than me."
"There are," his partner assured him,
"but they're no longer playing."

AUTHOR UNKNOWN

The latest statistical survey of golfers' height, conducted on behalf of a major sportswear company, reveals that the average player is seldom as tall as his stories.

AUTHOR UNKNOWN

The truly great things happen when a genius is alone. This is true especially among golfers.

J. R. COULSON

Fluff:

A shot in which the club head strikes the ground behind the ball before hitting it, causing it to dribble forward one or two yards.

A more widely used term for this type of stroke is "practice swing".

HENRY BEARD AND ROY MCKIE

Although golf was originally
restricted to the wealthy
and overweight,
today it's open to anybody who
owns hideous clothing.

DAVE BARRY

The object of a bunker trap
is not only to punish
a physical mistake,
to punish lack of control,
but also to punish pride
and egotism.

CHARLES BLAIR MCDONALD

Practice Tee:

The place where golfers
go to convert a nasty hook
into a wicked slice.

HENRY BEARD AND ROY MCKIE

The most important sho

If only I had taken up golf earlier
and devoted my whole time to it
instead of fooling about
writing stories and things,
I might have got my handicap down
to under eighteen.

P. G. WODEHOUSE

I'd like to see the fairways
more narrow.
Then everybody would have to
play from the rough, not just me.

SEVERIANO BALLESTEROS

n golf is the next one.

BEN HOGAN

Golf Ball:

A small object that remains
on the tee while a perspiring citizen
fans it vigorously with a large club.

AUTHOR UNKNOWN

When he gets the ball into
a tough place, that's when
he's most relaxed.
I think it's because he has so much
experience at it.

DOV CHRISTOPHER

I regard golf as an expensive way
of playing marbles.

G. K. CHESTERTON

Golf is a game
whose aim is to hit
a very small ball
into an even smaller hole,
with weapons singularly
ill-designed
for the purpose.

SIR WINSTON CHURCHILL

What other sport holds out
hope of improvement to a man
or woman over fifty?
For a duffer like the above-signed,
the room for improvement
is so vast that three lifetimes
could be spent roaming
the fairways carving away at it,
convinced that perfection
lies just over the next rise.

JOHN UPDIKE

Golf: A day spent in a round of strenuous idleness.

WILLIAM WORDSWORTH

I don't care to join any club that's prepared to have me as a member.

GROUCHO MARX

Give me a man with big hands,
big feet, and no brains
and I will make a golfer out of him.

WALTER HAGEN

Talking to a golf ball
won't do you any good,
unless you do it while
your opponent is teeing off.

BRUCE LANSKY

The only way
I could have beaten him was if
he fell into a lake and couldn't swim.

GEORGE BAYER

I see your golf
is improving.
You are missing
the ball much closer
than you used to.

LEOPOLD FECHTNER

I showed up but m

Golfball:

a sphere made of rubber bands
wound up about half as tensely
as the man trying to hit it.

AUTHOR UNKNOWN

golf game didn't.

BETH DANIEL

A wife always knows when
her husband has had a bad round.
He has pond weed in his socks.

PAM BROWN

Local rule at the Nyanza Golf Club:
If a ball comes to rest in
dangerous proximity to
a hippopotamus or crocodile,
another ball may be dropped
at a safe distance,
no nearer the hole, without penalty.

AUTHOR UNKNOWN

Years ago we discovered the exact point,
the dead center of middle age.
It occurs when you are too young
to take up golf
and too old to rush up to the net.

FRANKLIN P. ADAMS

If you pick up a golfer
and hold it close to your ear,
like a conch shell, and listen –
you will hear an alibi.

FRED BECK

The trouble that most of us find
with the modern matched
sets of clubs is that they don't really
seem to know any more about the game
than the old ones did!

ROBERT BROWNING

Love and putting are mysteries
for the philosopher to solve.
Both subjects are beyond golfers.

TOMMY ARMOUR

Golf:

A game in which you claim
the privileges of age, and retain
the playthings of childhood.

DR. SAMUEL JOHNSON

Few pleasures on earth match
the feeling that comes from
making a loud bodily-function noise
just as a guy is about to putt.

DAVE BARRY

Man blames fate
for other accidents
but feels
personally responsible
for a hole in one.

MARTHA BECKMAN

My score in golf
is in the low 70's –
before I reach the sixth hole.

PETER GRAY

Hook:

the addiction of fifty percent of golfers.

Slice:

the weakness of the other half.

JIM BISHOP

When you get up there
in years, the fairways
get longer and the holes
get smaller.

BOBBY LOCKE

A professional will tell you
the amount of flex you need
in the shaft of your club.
The more the flex,
the more strength you will need
to break the thing over your knees.

STEPHEN BAKER

A bad attitude is wors

Hope:
"Okay, what's wrong with my game?"
Palmer:
"If you're talking about golf,
that's not your game."

ARNOLD PALMER AND BOB HOPE

than a bad swing.
PAYNE STEWART

If you ever feel sorry for somebody
on a golf course, you better go home.
If you don't kill them,
they'll kill you.

SEVERIANO BALLESTEROS

Never smash a club
over your opponent's head.
You can't replace it
under the fourteen club rule.

HELEN THOMSON

I may be the only golfer
never to have broken
a single putter,
if you don't count the one
I twisted into a loop
and threw into a bush.

THOMAS BOSWELL

Nobody ever cheats
anybody else at golf.
The one who is cheated
is the one who cheats.

TOMMY ARMOUR

Golf is a game where guts,
stick-to-itiveness and blind devotion
will always get you absolutely nothing
but an ulcer.

TOMMY BOLT

If you wish to hide your character,
do not play golf.

PERCY BOOMER

My golf is improving. Yesterday I hit the ball in one!

PAM BROWN

I'm about five-inches from being an outstanding golfer. That's the distance my left ear is from my right.

BEN CRENSHAW

After the final, or eighteenth hole,
the golfer adds up his score and stops
when he has reached eighty-seven.
He then has a swim,
a pint of rye, sings "Sweet Adeline"
with six or eight other liars
and calls it the end of a perfect day.

AUTHOR UNKNOWN

Willis' Rule of Golf: You can't lose an old golf ball.

JOHN WILLIS

Golf instruction books can be
immensely valuable to the novice.
What you do is balance it
on top of your head and then
swing the club as hard as you can.
Once you have mastered the art
of taking the full vicious swing
without dislodging the book,
you can play golf.

PETER DOBEREINER

The best place to refine your swing
is, of course, right out on the
practice range…
You will have an opportunity
to make the same mistakes over
and over again
so that you no longer have to think
about them, and they become
part of your game.

STEPHEN BAKER

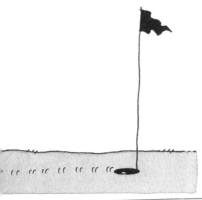

In primitive societies
they call it witchcraft when
the local tribes beat the ground
with clubs.
In civilised society it's called golf.

O. CUPIDO

Only religious ceremonies
proceed with more respect
than the major golf tournaments
in this country.

JIMMY CANNON

Fairway:

A narrow strip of mown grass
that separates two groups of golfers
looking for lost balls in the rough.

HENRY BEARD AND ROY MCKIE

Golf is a game in which
the slowest people in the world
are those in front of you,
and the fastest are those behind.

AUTHOR UNKNOWN

It is a law of nature that everybody plays
a hole badly when going through.

BERNARD DARWIN

The older I get the better I used to be.

LEE TREVINO

Golf clubhouse employees are
a carefully trained lot.
Take this locker-room boy for instance.
One Saturday evening he answered
the telephone and a female voice said,
"Is my husband there?"
The boy answered promptly, "No Ma'am."
"How can you say he isn't there
before I even tell you who I am?"
"Don' make no difference, Lady.
They ain't never nobody's husband here."

SEYMOUR DUNN

The oldest member of our golf club came into the club-house after his usual six holes and complained that he couldn't get out of the bunkers as well as he once could. His listeners suggested a number of possible remedies, but the old man shook his head. "It's not the ball that troubles me," he explained sadly, "It's getting myself out."

MAJOR C. GIBSON

Golf is a lot of walking, broken up by disappointment and bad arithmetic.

AUTHOR UNKNOWN

Sometimes you'd like to just stand there in the middle of the green and scream as loud as you can. But we're the perfect gentlemen.

RAYMOND FLOYD

The only thing that counts in golf
is the final number on the scorecard.
I always keep my own score.
I mark it correctly, to the best
of my knowledge.
But with all the strokes
I take on a hole,
I think I can be forgiven
if I forget one... or two...
but one time I went too far.
I made a hole in one
and marked down a zero.

BOB HOPE

One reward golf has given me,
and I shall always be
thankful for it,
is introducing me
to some of the world's most
picturesque, tireless
and bald-faced liars.

REX LARDNER

A ball will always
come to rest halfway
down a hill,
unless there is sand
or water at the bottom.

HENRY BEARD

A ball will always
travel farthest when hit in the
wrong direction.

AUTHOR UNKNOWN

The worse your drive
is stymied,
the more perfectly
it would have played
on the previous hole.

AUTHOR UNKNOWN

I know I'm getting
better at golf
because I'm hitting
fewer spectators.

GERALD R. FORD

My handicap?

If God had wanted humans to play golf he would have given him an elbow less left arm, short asymmetrical legs with side-hinged knees, and a trapezoid rib cage from which diagonally jutted a two-foot neck topped by a three-eyed head.

ALAN COREN

Woods and irons.

CHRIS CODIROLI

If profanity had an influence on the flight of the ball, the game would be played far better than it is.

HORACE G. HUTCHINSON

Reverse every natural instinct
and do the opposite of
what you are inclined to do,
and you will probably
come very close to having
a perfect golf swing.

BEN HOGAN

The difference between learning
to play golf and learning to
drive a car is that in golf
you never hit anything.

AUTHOR UNKNOWN

Being left-handed
is a big advantage.
No one knows enough
about your swing
to mess you up with advice.

BOB CHARLES

I find it more satisfying
to be a bad player at golf.
The worse you play,
the better you remember
the occasional good shot.

NUBAR GULBENKIAN

I don't need practice

Water holes are sacrificial waters
where you make
a steady gift of your pride
and high-priced balls.

TOMMY BOLT

I need a miracle.

BRUCE ASHWORTH

Golf is probably the only known
game a man can play as long
as a quarter of a century
and then discover it was too deep
for him in the first place.

SEYMOUR DUNN

I can airmail
the golf ball,
but sometimes
I don't put the
right address on it.

JIM DENT

A ball hit to the wrong green
will always
land two feet from the hole.

AUTHOR UNKNOWN

I'd give up golf if I didn't
have so many sweaters.

BOB HOPE

The greater the bet,
the longer the
short putts become.

AUTHOR UNKNOWN

I've thrown or broken a few clubs
in my day. In fact, I guess
at one time or another
I probably held distance records
for every club in the bag.

TOMMY BOLT

It took me seventeen years
to get 3000 hits in baseball.
I did it in one afternoon
on the golf course.

HANK AARON

For most amateurs,
the best wood
in the bag
is the pencil.

CHI CHI RODRIGUEZ

The reason the pro
tells you to keep your head down
is so you can't see him laughing.

PHYLLIS DILLER

Sneaky little devil, Polts.
Thought he was just a terrible player...
But he's laid a lawn front
and back of his new bungalow,
entirely of divots.

J. R. COULSON

I'm the best. I jus

I used to play golf with a guy
who cheated so badly
that he had a hole-in-one and wrote
down zero on his scorecard.

BOB BRUCE

haven't played yet.

MUHAMMAD ALI

The practice putting green
is either half as fast or twice
as fast as all the other greens.

AUTHOR UNKNOWN

Why, during those early days
Palmer was on tour, he threw them.
I have to say that he was the very
worst golf-club thrower
I have ever seen. He had to
learn to play well, he'd have
never made it as a thrower.

TOMMY BOLT

I have a tip
that can take five strokes off
anyone's golf game.
It's called an eraser.

ARNOLD PALMER

In prehistoric times, cavemen
had a custom of beating the ground
with clubs and uttering
spine-chilling cries.
Anthropologists call this
a form of primitive self-expression.
When modern men go
through the same ritual,
they call it golf.

HERBERT V. PROCHNOW AND
HERBERT V. PROCHNOW JNR.

Watching The Masters on CBS
is like attending a church service.
Announcers speak in hushed,
pious tones, as if to convince us
that something of great meaning
and historical importance
is taking place.
What we are actually seeing
is grown men hitting little balls
with sticks.

TOM GILMORE

It's that you lose nerves,
not nerve. You can quiver
like a leaf and fall
flat over a two foot putt.

JOHNNY FARRELL

People who would face torture
without a word become blasphemous
at the short fourteenth.

A. P. HERBERT

The ardent golfer
would play Mount Everest if somebody
put a flagstick on top.

PETER DYE

Golfers don't fist fight.
They cuss a lot.
But they wouldn't punch anything
or anybody. They might
hurt their hands and have to change
their grip.

DAN JENKINS

The more your opponent stresses
the importance of etiquette,
the better the odds that he will
sneeze in your backswing.

AUTHOR UNKNOWN

Competitive golf is
played mainly on a
five-and-a-half-inch course,
the space
between your ears.

BOBBY JONES

Apart from the adult who still
puts his Christmas present list up
the chimney, or a tooth under his pillow,
there is no one more gullible
than the average club golfer.

MARTIN JOHNSON

There is no movement
in the golf swing
so difficult that it cannot
be made even more difficult
by careful study
and diligent practice.

AUTHOR UNKNOWN

One thing that's always available
on a golf course is advice.
If you play like I do, you think everybody
knows something you don't know.
If I see a bird fly over, I think he's
going to tell me something.

BUDDY HACKETT

One philosopher had this to say about golf: "By the time you can afford to lose a ball, you can't hit it that far."

VIC FREDERICKS

My game is so bad I gotta hire three caddies – one to walk the left rough, one for the right rough, and one down the middle. And the one in the middle doesn't have much to do.

DAVE HILL

There is a saying around north Georgia that the Augusta National Golf Club is the closest thing to heaven for a golfer – and it's just about as hard to get into.

JOE GESHWILER

The real trick of golf course architecture is to lure the golfer into a false sense of security.

PETER DYE

The secret of missing a tree is to aim straight at it.

MICHAEL GREEN

The shortest distance
between any two points
on a golf course is a straight
line that passes directly
through the trunk
of a very large tree.

The divorce is from my old putter.
I think it's final – at least we're due
for a long separation. I've suffered
with that old putter for two years now.
It got so rude I couldn't stand it.

SHELLEY HAMLIN

What is Love compared with
holing out before your opponent?

P. G. WODEHOUSE

Whatever you leave out of your bag
is the one thing you will need –
if it is Band-aids,
you will develop a blister;
if it is a spare glove, yours will tear
on the fifth hole.

AUTHOR UNKNOWN

At least he can't cheat on his score –
because all you have to do
is look back down the fairway
and count the wounded.

BOB HOPE

The world's worst golfer hit his ball
into a monstrous bunker.
"What club should I use now?"
he wailed to his caddie.
"What club you use isn't important,"
answered the young man.
"Just take along plenty of food and water."

STEVE KEUCHEL

You know you're having a good day
when the course pro introduces you
to a tennis instructor.

RICHARD MINTZER

Golf increases the blood pressure, ruins the disposition, spoils the digestion... hurts the eyes, callouses the hands, ties kinks in the nervous system, debauches the morals, drives us to drink...

DR. A.S. LAMB

My worst day on the golf course still beats my best day in the office.

JOHN HALLISEY

Tell people you're taking up golf and you get one of two fairly predictable reactions. Those who have already been converted to the sport give you a punch on the arm or a whack on the back and say, with no hint of irony – there is no irony in golf – "Welcome to the clubhouse." Those who aren't converts, and who never will be, look at you with the sort of withering, pitying sneer that Shrek always gives Eddie Murphy's Donkey. Don't be fooled by the converted, though, as they're not your friends. They can smell fresh blood and are only waiting to get you out on to their favourite course in order to thrash you comprehensively.

DYLAN JONES

The green is,
in the golf religion,
the counterpart of
the sanctuary,
which surrounds
the cup or hole
which is, in golf,
the sacrosanct
equivalent of the altar.

JOHN MARSHALL

Most of us are egotistical enough
to believe that when we do something
badly it's really not our fault.
This is especially true of golf.
The tendency is to blame it on the
equipment, an incompetent caddie,
your wife's mother (who came to visit
one night and stayed three months),
or the fact that your clubs
were out of alignment,
or the grounds keeper hadn't been
putting enough manure
on the putting greens.

GROUCHO MARX

Your financial cost can best
be figured out when you realise
that if you were to devote the same time
and energy to business instead of golf,
you would be a millionaire
in approximately six weeks.

BUDDY HACKETT

On a recent survey,
eighty percent of golfers
admitted cheating.
The other
twenty percent lied.

BRUCE LANSKY

What the nineteenth hole proves
beyond a shadow of a doubt
is that the Scots invented
the game solely in order
to sell their national beverage
in large quantities.

MILTON GROSS

The only time you play great golf
is when you are doing everything within
your power to lose to your boss.

AUTHOR UNKNOWN

I was lying ten and had a thirty-five-foot
putt. I whispered over my shoulder:
"How does this one break?"
And my caddie said, "Who cares?"

JACK LEMMON

Every time I have the urge
to play golf I lie down
until the urge passes.

SAM LEVENSON

Golf does not discard people in the ruthless fashion of other more violent pursuits, and although a man's skill and strength may be declining he still has standards to aim at; he can continue to live in hope, perhaps for the rest of his days.

PAT WARD-THOMAS

The most exquisitely
satisfying act is
throwing a club.
The full back swing,
the delayed wrist action,
the flowing follow-through,
followed by that unique
whirring sound, reminiscent
only of a passing flock
of starlings, are
without parallel in sport.

HENRY LONGHURST

No one has ever
conquered this game.
One week out there
and you are a god;
next time you are the devil.

TIMOTHY LEARY

The more
you play it,
the less
you know
about it.

PATTY BERG

The sport of golf is everywhere,
but it is a relatively small world
at the top. A large tribe with a few,
highly trained warriors,
who go into the field accompanied
by their shield-bearers,
the caddies, to join battle armed
with only clubs and balls.

SEVERIANO BALLESTEROS

The more I practice

It is almost impossible to remember
how tragic a place this world is
when one is playing golf.

ROBERT LYND

the luckier I get.

GARY PLAYER

To the comedian,
George Burns:
"George, you look perfect…
that beautiful knitted shirt,
an alpaca sweater,
those expensive slacks…
You've got an alligator bag,
the finest matched irons,
and the best woods money
can buy. It's a damned shame
you have to spoil it
all by playing golf.

LLOYD MANGRUM

No game designed to be played
with the aid of personal servants
by right-handed men
who can't even bring along
their dogs can be entirely good
for the soul.

BRUCE MCCALL

Indeed, the highest pleasure
of golf may be that on the fairways
and far from all the pressures
of commerce and rationality,
we can feel immortal for a few hours.

COLMAN MCCARTHY

Golfer:
"I've never played
this poorly before."
Caddie:
"You've played before?"

FRED METCALF

You know you're having
a bad day when...
– You spend the majority of your day
ripping the cellophane off new balls.
– You've lifted your head
so often you have a crick
in your neck.
– The rest of your foursome
huddles behind a bench
as you tee off.
– Your tee-off time for tomorrow
has been revoked.
– Your club membership
has been revoked.

RICHARD MINTZER

Golf is the cruellest of sports.
Like life, it is unfair.
It's a harlot. A trollop. It leads you on.
It never lives up to its promises.
It's not a sport.
It's an obsession.
A boulevard of broken dreams.

JIM MURRAY

If you watch a game, it's fun.
If you play it, it's recreation.
If you work at it, it's golf.

BOB HOPE

There is one thing in this world that is dumber than playing golf. That is watching someone else play golf... What do you actually get to see? Thirty-seven guys in polyester slacks squinting at the sun.

Doesn't that set your blood racing?

PETER ANDREWS

I'm not playing golf with that
McPherson again. The man's a cheat.
How could he find his lost ball
a yard from the hole
when it was in my pocket
all the time?

AUTHOR UNKNOWN

Golf is balm. Even whe

The number of shots taken by
an opponent who is out of sight is
equal to the square root of the sum
of the number of curses heard
plus the number of swishes.

MICHAEL GREEN

t is driving us barmy.

SUE MOTT

A hole-in-one is an occurrence
in which a ball is hit directly
from the tee into the hole on a
single shot by a golfer playing alone.

ROY MCKIE

The older you get, the stronger the wind gets; and it's always in your face.

JACK NICKLAUS

If you want to take long walks,
take long walks.
If you want to hit things with sticks,
hit things with sticks.
But there's no excuse for
combining the two and putting
the results on TV.

NATIONAL LAMPOON

When ground rules permit golfers
to improve the lie,
they can either move the ball
or change the story about the score.

AUTHOR UNKNOWN

If I died...
it meant I couldn't
play golf.
No way was I
giving up golf,
so I gave up drinking.

BOB HOPE

Golf is the most fun
you can have without
taking your clothes off.

CHI CHI RODRIGUEZ

Eric:
My wife says if I don't
give up golf
she'll leave me.
Ernie:
That's terrible.
Eric:
I know, I'm really
gonna miss her.

ERIC MORECAMBE AND ERNIE WISE

I guess there is nothing that will get your mind off everything like golf. I have never been depressed enough to take up the game, but they say you get so sore at yourself you forget to hate your enemies.

WILL ROGERS

I never learned anything from a match that I won.

BOBBY JONES

It had been one of those days. A jinxed round succeeded in making the scratch golfer look an absolute rabbit. Maddened, he bent a club across his knee, drowned his best putter in the water hazard, shook his fist at the sky and bellowed, "Come down here and fight fair!"

AUTHOR UNKNOWN

Make no mistake. That golf ball sitting there so innocently on a tee or a little tuft of grass is your mortal enemy. Left to its own sinister devices, it will go exactly where you don't want it to, and absolutely refuse to go where you do want it to. In fact, it will do anything in its power to thwart your wishes, undermine your confidence, and destroy your composure, because beneath that placid dimpled exterior seethes an inner core of unmitigated animosity for every golfer who has played the game.

LESLIE NIELSEN AND HENRY BEARD

...all the important lessons of life
are contained in the three rules
for achieving a perfect golf swing:

1. Keep your head down.
2. Follow through.
3. Be born with money.

P. J. O'ROURKE

He's hit it fat…
It will probably be short…
It just hit the front edge
of the green…
It's got no chance…
It's rolling but it will stop…
It's rolling toward the cup…
Well I'll be damned!

JIMMY DEMARET

What other people may find
in poetry or art museums,
I find in the flight of a good drive.

ARNOLD PALMER

At twenty-five,
I thought a course that wasn't
seven thousand yards long
was a joke. At fifty,
I thought there ought to be
a law against them.

CHARLES PRICE

I've bought these long-distance balls –
but all I do is hit them
even further into the rough!

HELEN THOMSON

"I have never played on
such a course in my life,"
complained a visitor
to his caddie.
"You left the course
twenty minutes ago, Sir"
said the caddie drily.
"You're half way ower
tae Strathyrum now."

SCOTTISH GOLFER

We learn so many things from golf –
how to suffer for instance.

BRUCE LANSKY

It's funny. You need a fantastic memory in this game to remember the great shots, and a very short memory to forget the bad ones.

GARY MCCORD

If God wants to produce the
ideal golfer then He should create
a being with a set of unequal arms
and likewise legs, an elbow-free
left arm, knees which hinge sideways
and a rib-less torso from which
emerges, at an angle of 45 degrees,
a stretched neck fitted
with one colour-blind eye
stuck firmly on the left side.

CHRIS PLUMRIDGE

It may be said especially that mankind
has always displayed a uniform
craving for the pastime of hitting
a ball with a stick.
With the savage races, an enemy's
head has taken the place of the ball,
but the principle is still the same.

SCOTIA ON GOLF

We were all born
with webbed feet and a golf club
in our hand.

OLD TOM MORRIS

Golf is a game in which perfection stays just out of reach.

BETSY RAWLS

My goal is to become filthy rich.
But obviously, that isn't going
to be in golf. I'm working
on a stock-market fraud.

GARY MCCORD

My goal this year is basically
to find the fairways.

LAURI PETERSON.

Golf is a fascinating game.
It has taken me nearly forty years
to discover that I can't play it.

TED RAY

Howard and Horace were playing golf
when, by the side of the tenth hole,
Horace suddenly stopped playing
and watched a hearse and funeral
procession drive slowly along
a nearby road. As he watched, he
lowered his head and took off his cap.
"That was very noble of you,"
said Howard.
"Not at all," replied Horace.
"A husband should always show some
respect when his wife dies."

AUTHOR UNKNOWN

The glorious thing is that thousands of golfers, in park land, on windy downs, in gorse, in heather, by the many sounding sea, enjoy their imbecilities, revel in their infirmities, and from failure itself draw that final victory – the triumph of hope.

R.C. ROBERTSON - GLASGOW

A passion,
an obsession,
a romance,
a nice
acquaintanceship
with trees,
sand,
and water.

BOB RYAN

My top shots are
the practice swing
and the conceded putt.
The rest can never be mastered.

LORD ROBERTSON

Golf sucks you in one day
and spits you out the next.

MARK NICHOLAS

Very proud of having walked around
with him for the first time,
Daddy's Little Angel couldn't
wait to tell everyone about it.
"My father is the best golfer
in the whole world,"
she claimed –
"he can play for hours
and hardly ever lets the ball
go into those little holes."

AUTHOR UNKNOWN

I am a slave

Golf, like measles, should be
caught young, for, if
postponed to riper years,
the results may be serious.

P. G. WODEHOUSE

Vardon:
"What on earth shall I take now?"
Caddie:
"Well, Sir, I'd recommend the 4:05 train."

HARRY VARDON

to golf. ENID WILSON

"How was your golf game, dear?"
asked Murray's wife.
"I was hitting the ball pretty well,
but my eyesight's gotton so bad
I couldn't see where the ball went."
"Look, you're seventy-five years old,
Murray," his wife explained.
"Why don't you take my brother
Ira along?"
"But he's eighty-five and doesn't even
play golf anymore,"
Murray protested.

"But Ira's got perfect eyesight.
He could watch your ball."
The next day Murray teed off,
with Ira looking on.
Murray swung,
and the ball disappeared down
the middle of the fairway.
"Did you see the ball?"
asked Murray. "Yep," Ira answered.
"Where is it?" yelled Murray,
peering off into the distance.
"I forget."

RICHARD LEDERER

If it goes right,
it's a slice.
If it goes left,
it's a hook.
If it goes straight,
it's a miracle.

T-SHIRT

I had just come off a bogey and so
I wasn't in a great mood when
I stepped on the tee. I wasn't even
thinking about making it.
It was a perfect yardage and I flagged it.
It looked pretty good in the air
and then landed about four feet short
and left of the hole and rolled
in the back of the cup.
I guess I played the break perfectly.

BRENDON TODD,
on making a 1 at the 17th hole, a day after he aced the same hole.

Practice your bunker game
to become more aggressive with it.
You don't have to look at it as being
in anticipation of your misses.

HARVEY PENICK

"Daddy," said the bright child,
accompanying her father
on a round of golf,
"why mustn't the ball
go into the little hole?"

HERBERT V. PROCHNOW AND
HERBERT V. PROCHNOW JNR.

If you are going to throw a club,
it is important to throw it
ahead of you, down the fairway,
so you don't have to waste energy
going back to pick it up.

TOMMY BOLT

If your ball lands
within a club's length
of a rattlesnake
you are allowed
to move the ball.

LOCAL RULE AT THE GLEN CANYON
COURSE IN ARIZONA

Golf is a terrible, hopeless addiction, it seems: it makes its devotees willing to trudge miles in any manner of weather, lugging a huge, incommodious and appallingly heavy bag with them, in pursuit of a tiny and fantastically expensive ball, in a fanatical attempt to direct it into a hole the size of a beer glass half a mile away. If anything could be better calculated to convince one of the essential lunacy of the human race, I haven't found it.

MIKE SEABROOK

Putting allows the touchy golfer
two to four opportunities
to blow a gasket in the short space
of two to forty feet.

TOMMY BOLT

No matter how far its shaft extends,
a ball retriever is always a foot
too short to reach the ball.

AUTHOR UNKNOWN

The man who blames
fate for other accidents,
feels personally
responsible when he
makes a hole in one.

AUTHOR UNKNOWN

The putting green is the most
prolific scene of what those
so scrupulous [soccer] players
would call ungentlemanly conduct,
but there are other occasions.
To stand too closely over
an opponent in a bunker
is either an act of utter
ghoulishness or implies an
offensive doubt of his veracity.

BERNARD DARWIN

These kids have it mighty soft today.
I recently heard
one of my members
say to his son:
"You're a golf bum.
Are you going to be content
to spend your life tramping
around the golf course?"
And the kid said:
"No, Pop. I've been meaning
to speak to you about buying
me my own golf cart."

SAM SNEAD

What's the best time to take up golf? I don't care if you're fifteen or fifty, the answer is still the same. Ten years ago.

LESLIE NIELSEN AND HENRY BEARD

Wife: You think so much of your golf game you don't even remember when we were married. Husband: Of course I do, my dear. It was the day I sank that thirty-foot putt.

HERBERT V. PROCHNOW AND HERBERT V. PROCHNOW JNR.

I didn't need to finish college
to know what golf was all about.
All you need to know
is to hit the ball,
find it and hit it again
until it disappears into the hole
in the ground.

FUZZY ZOELLER

I've built golf courses
and laid the irrigation system
just by teeing off.

LEE TREVINO

To his pupil:
"You've just
one problem.
You stand too close
to the ball –
after you've hit it."

SAM SNEAD

Water creates a neurosis in golfers.
The very thought of this harmless
fluid robs them of their normal
powers of rational thought,
turns their legs to jelly, and produces
a palsy of the upper limbs.

PETER DOBEREINER

I'm using a new putter
because the old one
didn't float too well.

CRAIG STADLER

Just how childlike golf players
become is proven by their
frequent inability to count past five.

JOHN UPDIKE

Golfers find it a very trying matter
to turn at the waist,
more particularly if they have
a lot of waist to turn.

HARRY VARDON

I think most of the rules
of golf stink.
They were written by guys
who can't even break a hundred.

CHI CHI RODRIGUEZ

It's good sportsmanship
to not pick up lost balls
while they are still rolling.

MARK TWAIN

If you think it's hard
to meet new people,
try picking up the wrong golf ball.

JACK LEMMON

Golf is a game
where when you
don't succeed,
you try, try again.
And if you're honest,
you mark it down
on the score card.

SEYMOUR DUNN

My swing
is so bad,
I look like
a caveman
killing
his lunch.

LEE TREVINO

The person I fear most
in the last two rounds is myself.

TOM WATSON

My car absolutely
will not run unless
my golf clubs are in the trunk.

BRUCE BERLET

aaagh!